SCHOLASTIC

READ & RESPOND

Bringing the best books to life in the classroom

Activities based on Oliver's Vegetables

By Vivian French

Recommended system requirements:
Windows: XP (Service Pack 3), Vista (Service Pack 2), Windows 7 or Windows 8 with 2.33GHz processor
Mac: OS 10.6 to 10.8 with Intel Core™ Duo processor
1GB RAM (recommended)
1024 x 768 Screen resolution
CD-ROM drive (24x speed recommended)
Adobe Reader (version 9 recommended for Mac users)
Broadband internet connections (for installation and updates)

For all technical support queries (including no CD drive), please phone Scholastic Customer Services on 0845 6039091.

Designed using Adobe Indesign
Published by Scholastic Education, an imprint of Scholastic Ltd
Book End, Range Road, Witney, Oxfordshire, OX29 0YD
Registered office: Westfield Road, Southam, Warwickshire CV47 0RA

Printed and bound by Ashford Colour Press
© 2016 Scholastic Ltd
1 2 3 4 5 6 7 8 9 6 7 8 9 0 1 2 3 4 5

British Library Cataloguing-in-Publication Data
A catalogue record for this book is available from the British Library.
ISBN 978-1407-16059-7

Extracts from *The National Curriculum in England, English Programme of Study* © Crown Copyright. Reproduced under the terms of the Open Government Licence (OGL). http://www.nationalarchives.gov.uk/doc/open-government-licence/version/3

Due to the nature of the web, we cannot guarantee the content or links of any site mentioned. We strongly recommend that teachers check websites before using them in the classroom.

Author Sarah Snashall
Editorial team Rachel Morgan, Jenny Wilcox, Suzanne Adams, Rebecca Rothwell
Series designer Neil Salt
Designer Anna Oliwa
Illustrator Gemma Hastilow
Digital development Hannah Barnett, Phil Crothers and MWA Technologies Private Ltd

Acknowledgements
The publishers gratefully acknowledge permission to reproduce the following copyright material:

Hodder Children's Books for the use of extracts and cover from *Oliver's Vegetables* by Vivian French and illustrated by Alison Bartlett. Text © 1995, Vivian French. Illustration © 1989, Alison Bartlett. (1995, Hodder's Children's Book a division of Hachette Children's Books)

Every effort has been made to trace copyright holders for the works reproduced in this book, and the publishers apologise for any inadvertent omissions.

CONTENTS

INTRODUCTION

Read & Respond provides teaching ideas related to a specific children's book. The series focuses on best-loved books and brings you ways to use them to engage your class and enthuse them about reading.

The book is divided into different sections:

- **About the book and author:** gives you some background information about the book and the author.

- **Guided reading:** breaks the book down into sections and gives notes for using it with guided reading groups. A bookmark has been provided on page 10 containing comprehension questions. The children can be directed to refer to these as they read.

- **Shared reading:** provides extracts from the children's book with associated notes for focused work. There is also one non-fiction extract that relates to the children's book.

- **Phonics & spelling:** provides phonics and spelling work related to the children's book so you can teach these skills in context.

- **Plot, character & setting:** contains activity ideas focused on the plot, characters and the setting of the story.

- **Talk about it:** has speaking and listening activities related to the children's book. These activities may be based directly on the children's book or be broadly based on the themes and concepts of the story.

- **Get writing:** provides writing activities related to the children's book. These activities may be based directly on the children's book or be broadly based on the themes and concepts of the story.

- **Assessment:** contains short activities that will help you assess whether the children have understood concepts and curriculum objectives. They are designed to be informal activities to feed into your planning.

The activities follow the same format:

- **Objective:** the objective for the lesson. It will be based upon a curriculum objective, but will often be more specific to the focus being covered.

- **What you need:** a list of resources you need to teach the lesson, including digital resources (printable pages, interactive activities and media resources, see page 5).

- **What to do:** the activity notes.

- **Differentiation:** this is provided where specific and useful differentiation advice can be given to support and/or extend the learning in the activity. Differentiation by providing additional adult support has not been included as this will be at a teacher's discretion based upon specific children's needs and ability, as well as the availability of support.

The activities are numbered for reference within each section and should move through the text sequentially – so you can use the lesson while you are reading the book. Once you have read the book, most of the activities can be used in any order you wish.

Below are brief guidance notes for using the CD-ROM. For more detailed information, please click on the '?' button in the top right-hand corner of the screen.

The program contains the following:
- the extract pages from the book
- all of the photocopiable pages from the book
- additional printable pages
- interactive on-screen activities
- media resources.

Getting started

Put the CD-ROM into your CD-ROM drive. If you do not have a CD-ROM drive, phone Scholastic Customer Services on 0845 6039091.

- For Windows users, the install wizard should autorun; if it fails to do so then navigate to your CD-ROM drive. Then follow the installation process.
- For Mac users, copy the disk image file to your hard drive. After it has finished copying double click it to mount the disk image. Navigate to the mounted disk image and run the installer. After installation the disk image can be unmounted and the DMG can be deleted from the hard drive.
- To install on a network, see the ReadMe file located on the CD-ROM (navigate to your drive).

To complete the installation of the program you need to open the program and click 'Update' in the pop-up. Please note – this CD-ROM is web-enabled and the content will be downloaded from the internet to your hard drive to populate the CD-ROM with the relevant resources. This only needs to be done on first use; after this you will be able to use the CD-ROM without an internet connection. If at any point any content is updated, you will receive another pop-up upon start-up when there is an internet connection.

Main menu

The main menu is the first screen that appears. Here you can access: terms and conditions, registration links, how to use the CD-ROM and credits. To access a specific book click on the relevant button (note only titles installed will be available). You can filter by the

drop-down lists if you wish. You can search all resources by clicking 'Search' in the bottom left-hand corner. You can also log in and access favourites that you have bookmarked.

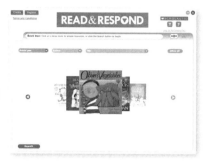

Resources

By clicking on a book on the Main menu, you are taken to the resources for that title. The resources are: Media, Interactives, Extracts and Printables. Select the category and then launch a resource by clicking the play button.

Teacher settings

In the top right-hand corner of the screen is a small 'T' icon. This is the teacher settings area. It is password protected and the password is: login. This area will allow you to choose the print quality settings for interactive activities ('Default' or 'Best') and also allow you to check for updates to the program or re-download all content to the disk via Refresh all content. You can also set up user logins so that you can save and access favourites. Once a user is set up, they can enter by clicking the login link underneath the 'T' and '?' buttons.

Search

You can access an all resources search by clicking the search button on the bottom left of the Main menu. You can search for activities by type (using the drop-down filter) or by keyword by typing into the box. You can then assign resources to your favourites area or launch them directly from the search area.

▼ CURRICULUM LINKS

Section	Activity	Curriculum objectives
Guided reading		Comprehension: To predict what might happen on the basis of what has been read so far.
Shared reading	1	Comprehension: To predict what might happen on the basis of what has been read so far.
	2	Comprehension: To explain and discuss their understanding of books.
	3	Comprehension: To discuss the sequence of events in books.
Phonics & spelling	1	Word reading: To read words containing taught GPCs and 's', 'es', 'ing', 'ed', 'er' and 'est' endings; to read words containing common suffixes.
	2	Word reading: To read common exception words, noting unusual correspondence between spelling and sound and where these occur in each word.
	3	Word reading: To respond speedily with the correct sound to graphemes, and to recognise alternative sounds for graphemes.
	4	Word reading: To read accurately words of two or more syllables.
Plot, character & setting	1	Comprehension: To discuss the sequence of events in books. Transcription: To learn the days of the week.
	2	Comprehension: To draw on their own experiences and vocabulary provided by the teacher.
	3	Comprehension: To be introduced to non-fiction texts that are structured in different ways.
	4	Comprehension: To make inferences on the basis of what is being said and done.
	5	Comprehension: To clarify the meaning of words and phrases.
	6	Comprehension: To explain clearly their understanding of what is read to them.
Talk about it	1	Spoken language: To give well-structured descriptions, explanations and narratives for different purposes, including for expressing feelings.
	2	Spoken language: To ask relevant questions to extend their understanding and knowledge.
	3	Spoken language: To maintain attention and participate actively in collaborative conversations, staying on topic and initiating and responding to comments.
	4	Spoken language: To articulate and justify answers, arguments and opinions; to participate in discussions and debates.
	5	Spoken language: To participate in a presentation.
	6	Spoken language: To participate in role play.
Get writing	1	Composition: To encapsulate what they want to say, sentence by sentence.
	2	Composition: To write narratives about those of others. Transcription: To add 'er' or 'est' to a root word.
	3	Composition: To write for different purposes.
	4	Composition: To learn how to use expanded noun phrases to describe; To write poetry.
	5	Composition: To write for different purposes.
	6	Composition: To write for different purposes.
Assessment	1	Comprehension: To discuss the sequence of events in books and how information is related.
	2	Transcription: To add 'er' or 'est' to a root word.
	3	Composition: To use expanded noun phrases to describe and specify.
	4	Composition: To write narratives about personal experiences and those of others.

About the book

Oliver's Vegetables by Vivian French, illustrated by Alison Bartlett, tells the gentle story of Oliver, who only eats chips. When Oliver goes to stay with his grandparents for a week, he strikes up a deal with his grandpa: if he can find the potatoes in his grandpa's garden, he can have chips; but if he finds any other vegetables he has to eat those without grumbling. Throughout the week, Oliver finds, eats and enjoys carrots, spinach, rhubarb, cabbage, beetroot and peas.

Oliver's Vegetables fits in perfectly with any unit on healthy eating and fun can be had trying and growing any of the vegetables in the book. It can also be used to discuss how things grow, grandparents, staying away from home, being brave, trying things, days of the week, colours and a healthy lifestyle. It lends itself to small-world play and work can be extended using the sequels *Oliver's Fruit Salad* and *Oliver's Milkshake*.

About the author

Vivian French (born 1945) started her career as an actor and a storyteller. Her first works were plays that she wrote for the travelling theatre company she belonged to. She has written over 250 books including *Oliver's Fruit Salad* and *Oliver's Milkshake*. She has written both books for teenagers and picture books for small children and likes the challenge of swapping between the two. She enjoys working with new illustrators and now runs a scheme to help new illustrators start their careers.

Vivian French was very unhappy at school but, like Oliver, would spend happy weeks staying with her grandparents and playing in their garden. Vivian French received an MBE in 2016 for services to literature and illustration. She lives in Edinburgh and has four grown up daughters and three grandchildren. Her favourite book is a blank notebook.

About the illustrator

Alison Bartlett was given *Oliver's Vegetables* to illustrate as part of a college assignment. After she exhibited the illustrations at the Macmillan Prize Exhibition in 1993 it was spotted by an agent. A year later, the book was published. She has continued to illustrate books for Vivian French and has gone on to illustrate books for numerous other authors. Her bright bold illustrations, full of colour, are always joyous. She lives in Bristol and has a young son.

Key facts

Oliver's Vegetables

Author: Vivian French

Illustrator: Alison Bartlett

First published: 1995 by Hodder Children's Books

Awards: Shortlisted for the Victoria and Albert Illustrator's Award

Did you know? Vivian French is in the top 25 of borrowed children's writers in British libraries.

GUIDED READING

Cover and predictions

Look together at the front cover and ask: *What do you think this story is going to be about?* (It is probably about a boy called Oliver and some vegetables.) Encourage the children to talk further about the predictions, for example, what might he be doing with the vegetables? Perhaps eating them? Perhaps cooking them? Perhaps growing them? Or selling them? Ask: *What vegetable is he holding on the front cover?* Agree that it is a bunch of carrots. Ask: *Has anyone seen carrots with the leaves still on? Does anyone know how a carrot grows?* Establish that the part we eat is the root and the green part is all that is seen above the ground.

Ask: *What vegetables do you like to eat? Who likes chips? What vegetable do chips come from?* Allow time for the children to talk about the different vegetables they eat and agree that chips come from potatoes. Read the back cover blurb. Ask: *Now what do you think is going to happen in the story?*

Before reading the story, pick out some of the vocabulary that you think that the children either will not know or will not be able to read, such as 'proudly', 'complaints', 'bargain', 'crinkly', 'helpings', 'tangle', 'delicious'. Display these words and read them together and discuss their meaning.

Spreads 1 to 3

Look together at the first spread. Ask: *What do we learn about Oliver on this page?* Allow time for the children to spot and discuss the cat, what Oliver is eating (and has left on his plate), what he says. Ask: *Do we know if Oliver is a healthy or an unhealthy boy?* Point out that he wants to walk to Grandpa's house – so perhaps he likes exercise more than vegetables. Ask: *How do you think Oliver feels?* Talk about the children's own experiences of staying away from home on their own. Turn the page and look together at the next two spreads with their

pictures of Grandpa's garden. Ask: *What is the garden like?* (It looks colourful, healthy and neat. It is described as 'wonderful'.) Ask: *What else can you see in Grandpa's garden?* (a shed, a bench, a dog, a greenhouse, a water butt) *What can we tell about Grandpa from his garden?* Perhaps that he loves gardening, he spends time out there, and so on. Talk about any gardens or allotments that the children's friends or relatives have.

Explain the meaning of the word 'bargain' on the third spread, and ask the children to discuss questions 1 to 3 on the Guided reading bookmark (page 10). Check that everyone understands what the bargain is and ask: *What do you think will happen? Will Oliver keep his side of the bargain? If he eats everything, do you think he will like everything?*

Spreads 4 to 8

Read the next spread. Ask: *How many carrots can you see on the page? Why can we only see the tops of five of them? In what way are they 'hiding'?* Look at spinach on the next page. Ask: *Is spinach really that big?* Ask: *What part of a spinach plant do we eat?* (the leaves) *What describing words are used to describe the spinach?* ('crinkly', 'pretty' and 'good') Turn to look at the rhubarb and talk about which part of the plant we eat and how. (We eat the stalks, which are cut up and cooked with sugar for puddings.) Look together at the next spread (Thursday) and ask: *How do we know that Oliver is not frightened of animals?* (He is always accompanied by the dog and he's happy to pick up the slug.) Pause for a moment ask the children to discuss question 8 on the Guided reading bookmark. Ask: *How do we know that Oliver likes cabbage?* He says so but he also has two helpings. Look at the beetroot on the next page. Ask: *How many 'very's does Oliver use?* (three)

Spreads 9 to 12

Look together at how Oliver finds the peas. (His football lands among them.) Ask: *How does Oliver find the potatoes?* (They are the only plants left.) *How does he help to make the chips?* (He scrubs the potatoes.) Ask: *Why do Gran, Grandpa and Oliver laugh when Mum arrives and is sad to see Oliver eating chips?* (Mum thinks Oliver's been eating chips all week and they know that these are the first he's eaten.)

Ask the children to turn to their partner and discuss questions 10 and 11 on the Guided Reading bookmark. Ask: *Why does he change his mind about vegetables?* Finally ask them to discuss question 12 on the bookmark with their partner.

Remind the children of their original predictions about the story and compare these with what happens. Ask the children to find Oliver's reactions to each of the meals he eats. Ask them to discuss questions 9 and 4 on the bookmark. Help them to see that Oliver becomes more and more enthusiastic about his meals as the story progresses. (His first comment, 'good', becomes 'very good', then, 'very, very good' then 'very, very, very good', then 'delicious'.)

Focus on structure

Ask the children question 5 on the Guided reading bookmark. Ask: *What is the event that starts off the story?* Agree that it is Oliver going to visit his gran and his grandpa suggesting the bargain. Ask: *What is the structure of the story?* (question 6 on the bookmark) Agree that the structure is the days of the week. Write the days of the week on the board and display media resources 'Growing vegetables'. Ask the children to work out what Oliver eats on each day of the week, matching the day to the photographs of vegetables. Talk about which the children know and like and which they have not eaten or do not like. Look at the pictures and talk about what part of the vegetable we eat and find this on the relevant page of *Oliver's Vegetables*. Compare the illustrations and the photographs. Ask: *Which do you prefer?* Ask the children to discuss question 7 on the bookmark. Create a vegetable patch on the classroom wall, encouraging the children to paint exuberant plants to stick on the wall in rows. Label each row and ensure that the children understand what each plant is.

■SCHOLASTIC
READ&RESPOND
Bringing the best books to life in the classroom

Oliver's Vegetables
by Vivian French

Focus on…
Meaning

1. Who are the main characters in the story?

2. What does Oliver eat at the beginning of the story?

3. What bargain does Oliver agree with his grandfather?

4. How does Oliver learn to love vegetables?

Focus on…
Organisation

5. What happens at the beginning of the story?

6. How is the story organised? (What is the structure of the story?)

■SCHOLASTIC
READ&RESPOND
Bringing the best books to life in the classroom

Oliver's Vegetables
by Vivian French

Focus on…
Language and features

7. What do you like about the illustrations?

8. What do you see the dog doing in the book?

9. What does Oliver say after each meal? Can you see a pattern?

Focus on…
Purpose, viewpoints and effects

10. What do you think about vegetables?

11. Why do you think Oliver never ate vegetables before?

12. What was your favourite part of the story? Why?

Extract 1

- Read Extract 1 on page 12 and clarify the meaning of 'bargain' and 'complaints'. Talk about the spelling of the long /ay/ sound in 'complaint' but not in 'bargain'.

- Ask: *Do you think that Oliver is going to keep his side of the bargain? How easy is it to try new vegetables (or new things)? Why are we scared to try new things? What clues are there that he will eat the vegetables?* (The title of the book; the use of 'wonderful' shows that Oliver is already interested in the garden; Oliver shakes hands on the deal.)

- Quickly locate the other long vowels: 'about', 'house', 'garden', 'I', 'grow', 'all', 'my', 'own', 'proudly', 'don't', 'eat', 'only', 'you', 'find', 'potatoes', 'no'. Circle the words and ask volunteers to underline the graphemes. Discuss the different spelling options.

- Ask: *What does Oliver think of the garden?* (It is 'wonderful'.) *What does Grandpa think of his garden?* (He is proud of it.)

Extract 2

- Read Extract 2. Help the children sound and blend 'tangle' and 'delicious'.

- Ask: *If Oliver arrived at Grandpa's on Monday, how long has he been there?* Recap on what he's eaten so far (carrots, spinach, rhubarb, cabbage and beetroot). Ask: *What has he thought of them?* ('good', 'very good', 'very, very good', 'very, very, very good').

- Ask the children to visualise the scene as Oliver climbs through the 'tangle' of peas. Ask someone with knowledge of growing peas to describe pea plants and their sticky, grabbing tendrils.

- Ask: *What can we tell about Oliver from this passage?* (Perhaps that he likes football, that he's not scared of pushing through undergrowth, that he likes to tease his Grandpa, he's being brave about trying new vegetables, happy to be outside.)

- Ask the children to circle the different endings: 's' in 'sticks', 'peas', 'leaves' and 'helpings'; 'es' in 'potatoes'; 'ed' in 'landed' and 'nodded' (pointing out the double 'dd' in 'nodded').

Extract 3

- Display Extract 3 and ask: *What does this text tell us?* (how a potato grows) Introduce the term 'non-fiction' and, if appropriate, 'explanation'.

- Ask the children to find five things about the text that are different from a story text (arrows, labels, diagram, numbered points, key words in bold).

- Read the key words and ask the children to speculate with a partner on what these words might mean and how to read them. Share ideas and clarify pronunciation and meaning.

- Challenge the children to locate key information from the text: *What do you need if you want to grow a potato? Where do the roots form? Where do the new potatoes form?* Ask: *Why can Oliver not find a potato when he first looks?* (They're under the ground.)

- Look at a potato together and ask the children to find the eyes on the potato and remember why these are important.

Extract 1

I don't eat vegetables

The best thing about Grandpa's house was the wonderful garden.

"I grow all my own vegetables," Grandpa said proudly.

"I don't eat vegetables," Oliver told Grandpa.
"I only eat chips."
"If you want chips," said Grandpa, "you must find the potatoes. If you find something else, you eat that and no complaints. Is it a bargain?"

Extract 2

Pea soup

On Saturday Oliver
played football.
The ball landed
in a tangle
of sticks and leaves.
Oliver was sure the
potatoes weren't there,
and Grandpa nodded.
"Peas," he said.
Oliver had three helpings
of pea soup that evening.
"Was that good?"
asked Grandpa.
"No," said Oliver,
"it was delicious!"

Extract 3

How a potato grows

This is how one potato can grow into lots of potatoes.

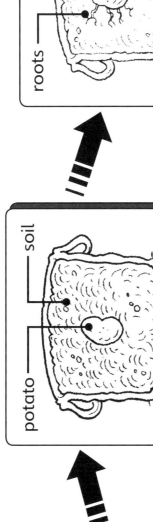

1. A single potato is planted in good soil.

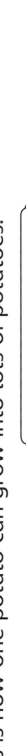

2. Roots and a stem grow out of the potato.

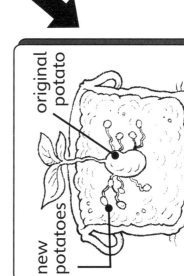

3. Small potatoes grow on the roots.

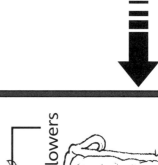

4. Flowers grow on the plant.

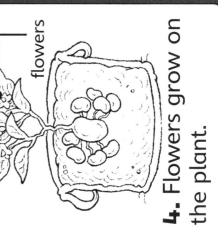

5. The potatoes are ready to harvest.

1. Jogged, jumped, rested

Objective

To read words containing taught GPCs and 's', 'es', 'ing', 'ed', 'er' and 'est' endings; to read words containing common suffixes.

What you need

Copies of *Oliver's Vegetables*, printable page 'Jogged, jumped, rested' and interactive activity 'Nod to nodded'.

What to do

- Ask the children to find and write down plurals from *Oliver's Vegetables*. Ask them to circle the ending in each word then hold up their boards.

- Agree that the ending is 's' in all cases apart from 'potatoes' which is 'es'. Correct any misconceptions over 'leaves' or 'vegetables'.

- Write the following words on the board: 'bushes', 'birds', 'tables', 'dishes', 'cups', 'watches', 'witches', 'apples', 'matches'. Link sound to spelling, pointing out the 's' (not 'es') ending in 'tables', 'leaves' and 'apples'.

- Now ask the children to find and write down words ending in 'ed' and then ask them to circle the ending. Share the words that the children have found and unpick the spelling of 'nodded' and 'hurried'.

- Ask: *How do we say the letters 'ed'?* Write 'jogged', 'jumped' and 'rested' on the board and agree that the ending 'ed' can be pronounced /d/, /t/ or /id/.

- Ask the children to complete printable page 'Jogged, jumped, rested'.

Differentiation

Support: Put these children in mixed-ability pairs to complete printable page 'Jogged, jumped, rested'. Ask the more confident learner to read the word aloud, allowing the less confident learner to make the decision about the pile.
Extension: Ask children to carry out interactive activity 'Nod to nodded' (which moves on to look at spelling).

2. Oliver's tricky words

Objective

To read common exception words, noting unusual correspondence between spelling and sound and where these occur in each word.

What you need

Printable page 'Oliver's tricky words'.

What to do

- Hand out copies of printable page 'Oliver's tricky words' to pairs of children. Ask the children to read each word in turn and discuss how the pronunciation of the word is different from the phonics rules they have learned. Encourage the children to turn to another pair for help with reading any words they are struggling with.

- Next ask them to underline or circle the letters that they are going to have to remember when reading or spelling these words.

- Provide the pairs with a second copy of the printable page. Tell them to cut out all the cards on the two sheets and use them to play a game of pairs. (Put all the cards face down and take turns to turn two over, keeping the cards if they are a pair. If you find a pair you get a second go. The winner has the most cards at the end of the game.) Remind them to say the words aloud as they turn over the cards.

- Finally, ask the children to use the cards as flashcards, testing each other on the spelling of the words.

Differentiation

Support: Spend time reading the words with children before they start the activity.
Extension: Give children a large grid and ask them to create a word search for the rest of the class using the words on the printable sheet.

3. Same letter – different sound

Objective

To respond speedily with the correct sound to graphemes, and to recognise alternative sounds for graphemes.

What you need

Copies of *Oliver's Vegetables*, individual whiteboards, printable page 'Same letter – different sound'.

What to do

- Ask the children to find words in *Oliver's Vegetables* with the grapheme 'oo'. Write the words on the board ('good', 'food', 'shook'). Ask volunteers to read the words and underline the 'oo' grapheme. Ask: *What sound does this grapheme make?* Agree that it makes a different sound in 'good' and 'shook' from the sound it makes in 'food'.

- Ask the children to work in pairs and give each pair two individual whiteboards. Ask the children to write 'good' on one board and 'food' on the other. Write the following words on the board and ask them to write the words on the small whiteboard that has the word with the matching vowel sound: baboon, roof, too, zoo, book, oops, hook, tool, wool, pool, foot, ooze, cook, mood, look, broom, hood.

- Hand out individual copies of printable page 'Same letter – different sound' and ask the children to complete the activity.

Differentiation

Support: Before they work independently, ensure the children can read: past, mast, grass; want, waddle; stamp, pack; also, go, so; drop, crock; Monday, smother. (Encourage them to use their own pronunciation of 'past', 'mast' and 'grass'.)
Extension: Provide children with two further circles labelled 'child' and 'trick' and ask them to write the following words in the circles to match the vowel sound: find, did, chips, mine, zip.

4. Long-word challenge

Objective

To read accurately words of two or more syllables.

What you need

Copies of *Oliver's Vegetables*, Extracts 1 and 2.

What to do

- Display an enlarged version of Extract 1 and start to read the passage out loud, pausing on the word 'wonderful'. Ask: *How do we attempt to read a long word such as this?* (Work out each sound in turn; split the word into wonder + ful; read each syllable won + der + ful). Discuss how we might use a different technique depending on how much of the word we know and how long it is. Explain that today you want them to practise breaking words into syllables and reading those.

- Write the following words on the board: 'garden', 'football', 'proudly', 'something' and 'complaints'. Ask volunteers to mark the syllable breaks and then read the words aloud (gar/den, foot/ball, proud/ly, some/thing, com/plaints). Ask who can spot a compound word in the list (football).

- Give pairs copies of Extract 2, or ask them to look at the spread in *Oliver's Vegetables*, and ask them to find seven longer words in the text, break them into syllables and read them (Sat/ur/day, veg/e/ta/bles, tan/gle, po/ta/toes, help/ings, eve/ning and de/li/cious).

- Provide the pairs with unfamiliar books at their reading level, and ask them to find words to attempt to read in this way. Share the words and discuss any unknown meanings.

Differentiation

Support: Provide children with a list of compound words to break down and read.
Extension: Challenge children to find three- and four-syllable words in their reading books.

1. Oliver's week

Objective

To discuss the significance of titles and events. To discuss the sequence of events in books. To learn the days of the week.

What you need

Copies of *Oliver's Vegetables*, media resource 'Growing vegetables', interactive activity 'Your daily vegetables', interactive activity 'Days of the week', fresh vegetables that appear in the book.

Cross-curricular link

Science

What to do

- Look at the photographs of the vegetables in media resource 'Growing vegetables', asking the children to describe them. If possible, bring in fresh examples and allow the children to investigate through touch. Cut the vegetables up so that the children can see inside, and explore the colour and texture together.

- Sort the vegetables (using printed versions of the photographs or the vegetables themselves) in different ways: green/other colours, grows under the ground/grows above the ground, used in sweet/savoury dishes. Can children think of other ways of sorting them?

- Organise the children to carry out interactive activity 'Your daily vegetables' in pairs. Provide them with copies of *Oliver's Vegetables* and tell them to work out what Oliver ate on which day.

- Then ask the children to do interactive activity 'Days of the week' to practise spelling the days of the week.

Differentiation

Support: Provide children with the days of the week as letters to rearrange.
Extension: Encourage children to write a sentence to describe each vegetable.

2. Healthy living

Objective

To draw on their own experiences and on vocabulary provided by the teacher.

What you need

(A week before you want to carry out this activity, ask the children to log everything they eat for a week to create their own food logs.) Food logs, media resource 'Healthy food plate', highlighting pens, printable page 'A healthy meal', interactive activity 'Balancing plates'.

Cross-curricular links

Design and technology, PSHE

What to do

- Display media resource 'Healthy food plate' and explain the food groups to the children.

- Talk about which foods fall into which groups.

- Provide the children with different coloured highlighters and work in groups to decide which food groups the foods in their food log are in. Hand out copies of printable page 'A healthy meal' and ask the children to put a tick in the correct section for each portion of food they've eaten for a week. Tell the children to share their 'A healthy meal' plate with a partner and decide together whether their week of food was healthy. Watch out for any food or home issues that might need to be supported sensitively.

- Ask the children to carry out interactive activity 'Balancing plates'.

- Ask: *Is Oliver's diet healthy before he visits Grandpa? Why not? Is his diet healthy when he is at Grandpa's?*

Differentiation

Support: Children will need adult support to fill in the healthy meal plate.
Extension: Ask children to write two sentences about how healthy their diet is.

3. Underground – over ground

Objective

To be introduced to non-fiction texts that are structured in different ways.

What you need

Printable page 'Overground – underground', photocopiable page 20 'Which part is the vegetable'?, media resources 'Growing vegetables' and 'Supermarket vegetables', examples of fresh vegetables.

What to do

- Ask: *Why does it take Oliver so long to find the potato?* (Because it's under the ground and he doesn't know what the leaves look like.) *How do we usually see potatoes?* (In the supermarket in bags). *Has anyone seen potatoes growing?*

- Hand out copies of printable page 'Overground – underground'. Ask: *Is this fiction or non-fiction? How do we know? Can you find any features of a non-fiction text?* (For example: introduction, heading, subheading, caption, pictures.) Ask the children to work in pairs to read the text.

- Hand out copies of photocopiable page 20 'Which part is the vegetable?' and ask the children to use the information from the printable page to label each plant and to circle the part that we eat.

- Display media resource 'Growing vegetables' to help the children identify them.

- Show the children the photographs in media resource 'Supermarket vegetables' or real examples of sweetcorn, apples, parsnips, cauliflower, red pepper and celery. Let the children investigate the fruit and vegetables in small groups and decide which part of a plant they are.

Differentiation

Support: Provide words for children to stick onto the photocopiable sheet.
Extension: Ask children to investigate and then explain how onions and garlic grow to the class.

4. Looking at Oliver

Objective

To make inferences on the basis of what is being said and done.

What you need

Copies of *Oliver's Vegetables*, photocopiable page 21 'Looking at Oliver'.

What to do

- Ask children to work in pairs and provide each pair with a copy of *Oliver's Vegetables*.

- Ask the children what they know about Oliver. Agree that we know that he only eats chips at the beginning of the book. Ask: *What else can we tell about Oliver from the book?* Tell the children to look through *Oliver's Vegetables* and see if they can find out anything else about Oliver. Help the children to find evidence in the text to show that he prefers walking to driving, he plays football, he likes visiting his grandpa and he keeps his word.

- Remind the children about previous work on verbs and ask volunteers to find some verbs in *Oliver's Vegetables*. Ask: *Who is doing the saying/asking/running in this sentence?* Locate the appropriate subject. Model finding verbs that explain what Oliver does in the story, such as 'ran', 'pulled', 'got up early', 'hurried', 'rushed' and 'laughed'.

- Hand out copies of photocopiable page 21 'Looking at Oliver' and ask the children to work in pairs to fill it in.

Differentiation

Support: Provide children with a list of verbs from the book plus others such as 'moaned', 'plodded', 'slept' and so on. Ask the children to find which are in the book.
Extension: Ask children to complete the sentence, 'I think Oliver is… because…'

5. New word challenge

Objective

To discuss word meanings, linking new meanings to those already known. To clarify the meaning of words and phrases.

What you need

Copies of *Oliver's Vegetables*, for each group: a dice, sets of word cards showing key words from the first three spreads (in a hat or bowl).

What to do

- On the board, write words from the book that were new to the children (such as 'beetroot', 'spinach', 'cabbage', 'rhubarb', 'crinkly', 'helpings', 'complaint', 'bargain' and 'tangle') and ask volunteers to explain what each means in turn. Look at the spelling of each word and point out any examples where the spelling and the pronunciation do not match in the way you would expect.

- Challenge the children to choose one of the words and say how it is important in the story.

- Organise the children into groups and give each group a hat or bowl with a set of words from the opening three spreads on separate cards, and a dice. Ask them to take turns to take a card out of the hat and roll the dice. Tell them to answer the correct question according to the number they roll:
  - 1 or 2: What does the word mean?
  - 3 or 4: How is it important to the story?
  - 5 or 6: Say a sentence using the word.

Differentiation

Support: Select words for these children that you think will be most useful to them.
Extension: Ask children working as a team to create a word card for each of the words. Hang these cards on a loop in the reading corner.

6. The vegetable patch

Objective

To explain clearly their understanding of what is read to them.

What you need

Copies of *Oliver's Vegetables*, media resources 'Growing vegetables', pencils, paper, coloured pencils, photocopiable page 20 'Which part is the vegetable?'.

Cross-curricular links

Science and art

What to do

- Hand out copies of *Oliver's Vegetables* and look together at the second spread which shows Grandpa's vegetable patch. Encourage volunteers to try and identify the vegetables from the story.

- Tell the children to draw their own version of Grandpa's vegetable patch. Display the photographs in media resource 'Growing vegetables' and provide the children with their filled-in versions of photocopiable page 20 'Which part is the vegetable?' for reference.

- Tell the children that the vegetable patch needs to have all seven vegetables in it and that they should try to draw the leaves as accurately as their drawing skills allow. Remind them that they will not need to show anything that is unseen under the ground, such as the carrots and potatoes, although the more creative might like to make a flap that will reveal what is under the earth.

- Ask the children to use fresh paper to create labels to stick on their drawing. Encourage them to create descriptive phrases, using vocabulary from the book if they want, for example: 'crinkly spinach', or their own vocabulary if they wish, such as 'delicious cabbage', 'rhubarb – great for making pies'.

Differentiation

Support: Provide a wide range of words for the children to choose from to label their picture.
Extension: Ask children to write a description of the vegetable patch.

Which part is the vegetable?

● Can you recognise these plants? Complete the caption for each one. Then circle the part of the plant we eat.

This is a _____ plant.

We eat the _____.

This is a _____ plant.

We eat the _____.

This is a _____ plant.

We eat the _____.

This is a _____ plant.

We eat the _____.

This is a _____ plant.

We eat the _____.

This is a _____ plant.

We eat the _____.

This is a _____ plant.

We eat the _____.

Looking at Oliver

- What do we know about Oliver? Use Oliver's *Vegetables* to look for clues. Write them in the boxes below.

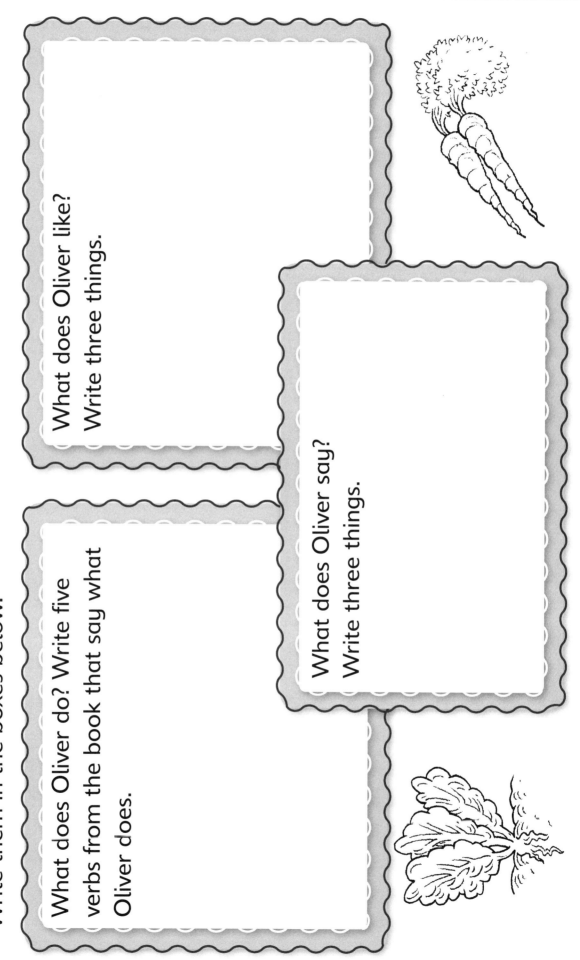

What does Oliver like?
Write three things.

What does Oliver say?
Write three things.

What does Oliver do? Write five verbs from the book that say what Oliver does.

▼ TALK ABOUT IT

1. What I like to eat

To give well-structured descriptions, explanations and narratives for different purposes, including for expressing feelings.

What you need

Photocopiable page 25 'My favourite meal' and a dice for each group.

Cross-curricular link

Design and technology

What to do

- Ask the children to work with a partner and take it in turns to pretend to be Oliver telling a friend about his food experience at his grandparents' house.

- Tell the children about a food memory you have. Model using adjectives and using structure and detail to create an interesting anecdote, for example: *Every summer my granny would take me to the seaside and buy me the most enormous ice cream. It came covered with nuts and strawberry sauce. It was so sweet and cold and creamy and sticky. It tasted better than any ice cream I've ever had since.*

- Organise the children into groups and give each group a copy of photocopiable page 25 'My favourite meal' and a dice. Tell them to take turns to throw the dice and talk about the subject in the corresponding speech bubble.

- Explain that they should try to say two or three sentences about the subject and use at least one adjective. Tell the groups to award themselves one point for each sentence and one point for each adjective and that they can encourage and help each other to talk further on the subject.

- Share the number of points and any anecdotes the groups would like to share.

Differentiation

Extension: Challenge children to create their own interesting anecdote.

2. Going on a visit

Objective

To ask relevant questions to extend their understanding and knowledge.

Cross-curricular link

PSHE

What to do

- Ask: *Why do you think Oliver goes to stay with his grandparents for a week?* (school holidays, his mum is working, for a treat and so on.)

- Tell the children about staying with a relative as a child, for example: *One summer my sisters and I stayed with an elderly aunt. She was terrifying and very strict and lay in state in a huge high bed. But when she was sleeping we ran riot in the house which had two staircases, numerous bedrooms and a rocking horse in the attic.*

- Tell the children to think about a time when they stayed overnight at someone else's house. Tell them to think about what they liked or disliked about the stay, what they did, who else was there, what they ate and how they felt.

- Next ask the children to get into pairs and take turns to ask each other questions about their overnight experience. Tell them they might want to think of questions that start 'How', 'What', 'Who', 'When', 'Where' and so on. Challenge them to find out as much about their partner's experience as possible.

- Question individual children about their partner's experience. Have they managed to learn some interesting facts? Can they talk about how their partner felt?

Differentiation

Support: Provide these children with a number of general questions to ask.
Extension: Challenge these children to ask interesting questions that really get their partner talking.

3. Planning a menu

Objective

To maintain attention and participate actively in collaborative conversations, staying on topic and initiating and responding to comments.

What you need

Media resource 'Healthy food plate', simple children's recipe books.

Cross-curricular links

Design and technology, PSHE

What to do

- Remind the children of the work they did on 'Healthy living' (see page 17) and display media resource 'Healthy food plate'.

- Organise the children into groups. Explain that, as a group, their task is to plan three healthy meals for a day (breakfast, lunch and dinner). Their menu needs to contain lots of fruit and vegetables but can also contain other items which should be eaten less often such as honey, meat, chips and so on, but in balance with the fruit and vegetables. Tell the children that they can have up to three dishes for each meal.

- Explain that this is a group project and that everyone needs to contribute. Remind them to listen to each other's ideas, making sure that something from everyone makes it onto the final menu. Tell them that you will listen out for such remarks as 'I like that idea…', 'Yes, that's a good plan…', 'Can we take that part of your idea and add…?'

- Provide the children with simple recipe books for inspiration if they are struggling.

- Challenge them to write their menu and decorate it.

Differentiation

Support: Provide pictures of different foods for these children to discuss and combine.
Extension: Challenge these children to write a description for each dish for their menu.

4. Slug and snail attack

Objective

To articulate and justify answers, arguments and opinions; to participate in discussions and debates.

What you need

Copies of *Oliver's Vegetables*, for each group a set of cards cut out from printable page 'Slug and snail attack'.

Cross-curricular link

Science

What to do

- Ask: *Can you remember which vegetable the slugs and snails were eating*? (cabbages)

- Ask: *Does it matter that the slugs and snails are eating Grandpa's cabbages? What should he do with them?* As the children give their opinions, point out possible objections ('That might be cruel', 'Grandpa loves cabbage', 'They are not always put off by gravel' and so on).

- Organise the children into groups of six and give each group member a different point-of-view card from printable page 'Slug and snail attack'. Challenge each child to persuade the group to the point of view of their card. Remind them of the rules of a group discussion. Give the groups a few minutes to discuss the different options, choosing one solution.

- If time, change cards. Will a different solution win this time?

- Carry out a 'conscience alley'. Ask the children to take turns to play Grandpa and walk through the alley as the children tell Grandpa what to do with the slugs and snails.

Differentiation

Support: Provide children with points to go with the card they are given. Practise talking about the subject before the session.
Extension: Tell children to investigate good ways of protecting plants.

5. Healthy eating is great!

Objective

To participate in presentations.

What you need

Media resource 'Healthy eating is great!', computer access or flipcharts.

Cross-curricular links

Design and technology, PSHE.

What to do

- Ask: *What do you think Oliver will want to say to his friends at school about eating vegetables?* Tell them that Oliver is so enthusiastic about eating vegetables that he has decided to give a presentation.

- Organise the children into groups and ask the groups to discuss the sort of things that Oliver would say in his presentation, for example, what we should eat, what sort of vegetables there are, how tasty they can be, other ways we can be healthy, and so on.

- Explain that the groups are going to give their own presentations on healthy eating. Show the children the presentation slides from media resource 'Healthy eating is great!' modelling how to complete the slides. Allow groups who do not want to use the presentation to make their own (on either the computer or using a flipchart).

- Help groups to organise who should say what and ensure all children are involved.

- Let the children take turns to give their presentations.

- Save the presentations for use later on.

Differentiation

Support: Organise for children to work in a mixed-ability group and ensure they are given a part in the presentation.
Extension: Encourage children to create their own presentation using a presentation package.

6. Oliver role play

Objective

To participate in role play.

What you need

Printable page 'Role-play cards' cut into cards.

What to do

- Organise the children into pairs and ask them to role play a conversation between Oliver and his mother just before they go to Gran and Grandpa's. Tell them that we know some of the things that Oliver says ('Can't we walk?') but they will have to imagine the other things, for example: 'Remember your manners', 'Eat everything you're given', 'Help to clear the table' and so on.)

- After a few minutes ask them to try another conversation with another partner, working on each for a few minutes:
  - Oliver and his mother
  - Oliver and his grandpa
  - Oliver and the dog (they can imagine the dog can speak!)
  - Oliver and his gran
  - Oliver and his mother on the day she picks him up
  - Oliver and a friend at school

- Encourage them to bring in everything they know about the characters and any other subjects discussed in class such as slugs and snails and healthy eating. Remind them that they can use speech from the story, as well as their own ideas.

- Provide children who need a bit of inspiration with the role-play cards from printable page 'Role-play cards'.

- Take each role play in turn and ask a pair of volunteers to share their role play.

Differentiation

Support: Work with children, helping them to formulate some lines to say.
Extension: Challenge children to attempt to write lines from one of their role-play conversations.

My favourite meal

- Roll a dice. Talk about the subject for the number you rolled.
- Try to say two or three sentences and include an adjective.

1 If you roll a one... talk about your favourite meal.

2 If you roll a two... talk about school dinners or what you have in your packed lunch.

3 If you roll a three... talk about which vegetables you like and which you don't.

4 If you roll a four... talk about the strangest food you've heard of.

5 If you roll a five... describe your favourite pudding.

6 If you roll a six... talk about a food memory.

GET WRITING

1. Poppy's exercise

To encapsulate what they want to say, sentence by sentence.

What you need

Photocopiable page 29 'Poppy's exercise', six speech-bubble shaped pieces of paper for each child who needs support.

What to do

- Tell the children to imagine that Oliver has a cousin called Poppy. Poppy loves her phone. All she wants to do is play on her phone – chatting to friends, listening to music and playing games. During the holidays, Poppy goes to stay with her friend Maya. Maya likes to spend all her time outside and over the course of the week Poppy finds out that it's fun to be sporty. However, on the last day it's raining and when Poppy's mum arrives, she's disappointed to see Maya and Poppy playing on Poppy's phone.

- Hand out copies of photocopiable page 'Poppy's exercise' and ask pairs to take turns to tell each other the story in their own words. Tell them to compose at least one sentence for each picture, using the key words if useful. Encourage them to use some of the features in *Oliver's Vegetables*, for example, Maya could ask Poppy what she thinks of each sport and she can be increasingly enthusiastic.

- When they are ready to write their story, remind them of the work done earlier on syllables. Model how this can be used to spell longer words they need such as ho/li/day or brill/i/ant.

Differentiation

Support: Provide children with speech bubbles to fill in and stick onto the pictures – one per scene.
Extension: Challenge children to add an adjective to three of the sentences.

2. Best in show

Objectives

To write narratives about personal experiences and those of others (real and fictional); to say out loud what they are going to write about; to add 'er' or 'est' to a root word.

What you need

Photocopiable page 30 'Best in show'.

Cross-curricular link

Art

What to do

- Explain that the children are going to write another story about Oliver. Display an enlarged version of photocopiable page 30 'Best in show' and together talk about what might happen in the story. Perhaps the prize pig eats Mr Topps' marrow, perhaps Gran has exhibited a cake that wins a prize, perhaps Grandpa accidently eats Gran's cake.

- Circle the endings in 'big', 'bigger', 'biggest'; 'fine', 'finer' and 'finest', and 'tasty', 'tastier' and 'tastiest'. Remind the children about previous work on endings. Agree that for some words you can just add the ending ('small' to 'smaller'); for words with a short vowel before one consonant we double the consonant ('big' to 'bigger'); for words ending in 'e' we just add 'r' ('fine' to 'finer') and finally for words ending in a 'y' we turn the 'y' into an 'i' before adding 'er' ('yummy' to 'yummier').

- Ask pairs to talk about what might happen before drawing a series of pictures for their story. Ask them to verbally compose a sentence for each drawing, checking that it makes sense before writing it down.

Differentiation

Support: Work with children to compose a relatively simple story to storyboard and write captions for.
Extension: Ask children to write a longer story, checking their spellings and adding further comparatives and superlatives.

3. Eat your veg

Objectives

To write for different purposes.

What you need

Copies of *Oliver's Vegetables*, poster-sized pieces of paper, media resource 'Healthy eating is great!' (saved copies of groups' presentations).

Cross-curricular link

PSHE

What to do

- Remind the children about the presentation they gave about eating healthily. Tell them that they are now going to create a poster.

- Discuss possible headings for their posters (though it doesn't need to be at the top of the page), for example: 'It's good to be green', 'Eat your veg', 'Healthy eating – healthy body', 'Let's be healthy', 'Eat well – stay well', 'Get your tasty five a day', 'Five a day to work, rest and play'.

- Suggest that the children choose one main image to draw or stick in the centre, then use smaller images with captions around the outside, for example: 'Eat fruit and vegetables of different colours'; 'Carrots are great raw'; 'Put an apple in your lunchbox'; 'Vegetable soup is delicious and good for you'. Challenge the children to use a word ending in 'er' or 'est' in their poster ('tastier', 'tastiest', 'healthier', 'healthiest', 'happier') and to use the word 'because' at least once.

- Provide the children with access to their 'Healthy eating is great!' presentations and copies of *Oliver's Vegetables* to inspire them.

- Once the children have finished their posters, display them in the dinner hall.

Differentiation

Support: Scribe for children, encouraging them to verbalise their ideas.
Extension: Encourage children to create a leaflet with more text – perhaps a recipe.

4. Poetic vegetables

Objective

To learn how to use expanded noun phrases to describe and specify; to write poetry.

What you need

(Beforehand, gain parental permission for food tasting and ascertain any food allergies in the class.) A large selection of fruit and vegetables, printable page 'Crunchy carrots' cut up into individual words.

Cross-curricular link

Design and technology

What to do

- Discuss the various fruit and vegetables you have brought in. Place each on a different table with a set of words from printable page 'Crunchy carrots' next to it.

- Tell the children to taste each fruit or vegetable in turn and choose a word from the pile to go by the fruit or vegetable. If the word they want has already been chosen, tell them to put a tick on the word.

- Glue the chosen words around a picture of each fruit or vegetable and display the sheets. Ask volunteers to use the sheets to create different noun phrases verbally, such as 'crunchy carrots', 'juicy oranges', 'purple beetroot' and so on.

- Ask the children to create a list poem of noun phrases. Suggest opening lines such as 'At the market I like to buy', 'Vegetables, vegetables – I love veg' or 'Let's get healthy, let's eat' and so on.

- Ask volunteers to read their poems.

Differentiation

Support: Provide children with their own set of the words from printable page 'Crunchy carrots' and cards for each vegetable to create and stick down their list.
Extension: Children could write further lines in their poems for vegetables not tried in class.

5. How to grow peas

Objectives

To write for different purposes.

What you need

Internet or library access, printable page 'How to grow peas'.

Cross-curricular link

Science

What to do

- Remind the children about the features of instruction texts: command or 'bossy' words ('dig', 'water', 'pick)', special vocabulary, numbered points, illustrations.

- Organise for small groups to work with an adult to research how to grow peas. Help them to make notes, writing down key words such as 'soil', 'water', 'seed', 'shoot', 'root', 'flower', 'seed pod' and so on.

- After the research, ask the children to tell you how to grow peas. Write the key words on the board as they come up. Write 'First', 'Then', Next', 'Finally' on the board and challenge volunteers to use these in their verbal sentences.

- Display an enlarged version of printable page 'How to grow peas' and ask different volunteers to come to the front and use the diagram to explain how to grow peas. Remind them to use the key words.

- Ask the children to complete printable page 'How to grow peas'.

- Once they've finished, ask them first to check their own set of instructions, then to swap with a partner and check theirs – tell them to look for key words, bossy words, time words and spelling.

Differentiation

Support: Provide children with text to stick down.
Extension: Ask children to add a 'Did you know' or 'Fact' box to the corner of the instructions and to use information from their earlier research.

6. Minibeast watch

Objective

To write for different purposes.

What you need

Printable page 'Minibeast watch', books about minibeasts, internet access.

Cross-curricular link

Science

What to do

- Provide the children with books about minibeasts and ask them to read about each of the six minibeasts they found in Grandpa's vegetable patch (slug, snail, caterpillar, bee, ladybird, beetle). Encourage them to work with a partner to find out one fact and think of one adjective for each minibeast, noting these down.

- Tell the children to share their facts and adjectives with another pair, writing any new information or adjectives they liked from the new pair.

- Provide the children with individual copies of printable page 'Minibeast watch' and ask them to write a noun phrase (for example, 'spotty ladybird') as a caption for each picture and to write a sentence as the fact for each picture (for example, 'Gardeners love ladybirds because they eat aphids.').

Differentiation

Support: Choose just two minibeasts for children to work on.
Extension: Ask children to investigate whether each minibeast is good or bad for the vegetable patch.

Poppy's exercise

- Use these pictures to write a story about Oliver's cousin Poppy who goes to stay with her sporty friend Maya. You can use the key words to help you.

Monday

phone, headphones, sporty, cycling, roller skating, tennis

Tuesday

cycling, sunshine, woods

Wednesday

tennis, rackets, picnic, park

Thursday

roller skating, park, laughing

Friday

raining, disappointed

Best in show

It was the end of August and Grandpa and Oliver were off to the produce show to show Grandpa's prize marrow. There were three prizes to be won at the show: Tastiest cake, Biggest marrow and Finest pig. Grandpa's marrow was very big but Mr Topps' looked enormous.

● Using the picture, write a story of the produce show.

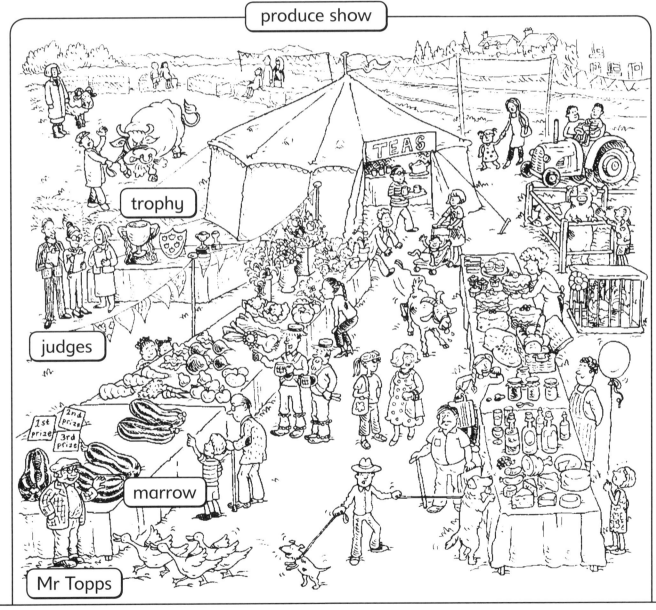

produce show

trophy

judges

1st prize
2nd prize
3rd prize

marrow

Mr Topps

Useful words: disaster, fine, finer, finest, tasty, tastier, tastiest, big, bigger, biggest, enormous, marrow

1. Oliver in order

Objective

To discuss the significance of titles and events; to discuss the sequence of events in books and how items of information are related.

What you need

Interactive activity 'Oliver in order', a copy of *Oliver's Vegetables.*

What to do

- Tell the children to turn to their partner and together remember the events of *Oliver's Vegetables.* Share the children's thoughts. Discuss that it is important that the potato is the last vegetable, but ask: *How would the story change if the order of the other vegetables was changed?* (Not at all but Oliver's response to the individual dishes would need to change so that he continues to get more and more enthusiastic about the food.)

- Organise for the children to carry out interactive activity 'Oliver in order'. Tell them to order the sentences. When they have them in the correct order ask them to copy each statement then write another sentence about what Oliver thinks, or how he reacts to the vegetables on a piece of paper.

- Move on to assess the children's understanding of the book in general by asking them to write a back-cover blurb for the book (without letting them see the one on the actual book). Tell them the blurb should give a taste of the book, covering the main idea, but without giving the whole plot.

- Share the children's blurbs and then read the one on the book. Which do they prefer?

Differentiation

Support: Create a paper version of 'Oliver in order' for the children to stick down in order with captions provided.
Extension: Ask children to write a review of *Oliver's Vegetables.*

2. Only the best

Objective

To add 'er' or 'est' to a root word.

What you need

Interactive activity 'Only the best', media resource 'Growing vegetables'.

What to do

- Ask the children to carry out interactive activity 'Only the best'. The first screen of this activity only requires the children to add 'er' or 'est' endings; the second screen requires them to change the spelling of the root word as well in some cases.

- Share the words that the children have written, correcting any mistakes.

- For further assessment if required, display the images of vegetables from media resource 'Growing vegetables' and ask the children to write a sentence using a word ending in 'er' or 'est' as a caption for each (for example: 'Spinach has the greenest leaves.' 'Celery is the crunchiest food in my lunch box.').

- Provide the following captions for less confident learners and ask them to stick the caption next to the picture and circle the 'er' or 'est' ending:
  - Sweetcorn is easier to eat if you take it off the cob.
  - We have the sweetest apples in our garden.
  - My sister makes the cheesiest, creamiest cauliflower cheese.
  - Red peppers are nicer than green peppers.
  - Celery is even stringier than old green beans.

Differentiation

Support: Ask children to focus only on the first screen.

3. Healthy nouns

Objective

To learn how to use expanded noun phrases to describe and specify.

What you need

A bag of everyday objects (for example: bar of soap, pencil, spoon, photograph, book), interactive activity 'Healthy nouns'.

What to do

- Hold out the bag of objects and ask one person from each group or table to pick out an object. Tell the groups to work together to create a list of adjectives for their object and then use these to write a list of noun phrases (for example: 'pink soap', 'crumbly soap', 'creamy soap'; 'orange pen', 'useful pen', 'new pen').

- Swap objects and lists with a group. Challenge the new groups to add to the previous group's list of noun phrases.

- Ask the children to work individually to match adjectives to nouns on the interactive activity 'Healthy nouns'. Explain that there is more than one answer and that they should be creative about their adjective and noun pairing, while still thinking about what the item is really like.

- Ask the children to remember some of the noun phrases from the interactive activity and to create some sentences including them.

- Encourage children to tell you about a healthy feast they had – or would like – at home. For example, 'I had a fluffy jacket potato with some creamy cheddar and crunchy coleslaw. For pudding I had some sharp apples with some gooey caramel sauce.'

Differentiation

Support: Provide children with nouns and adjectives to match together to form noun phrases.
Extension: Provide children with an image of a busy street scene and ask them to label the picture with noun phrases.

4. Dear Poppy

Objective

To write narratives about personal experiences and those of others (real and fictional). To learn the days of the week.

What you need

Copies of *Oliver's Vegetables*.

What to do

- Ask: *Who can remember the structure of* Oliver's Vegetables? (A different vegetable each day.) Tell the children to practise spelling the days of the week with a partner.

- Tell the children that they are going to be writing a letter to Poppy from Oliver in which he tells her all about the trip to Grandpa's. Remind them to start 'Dear Poppy' and to use the days of the week to talk about some (but not all) of the things that happened. Remind them that they will need to say 'I' for Oliver. Explain that they are not rewriting the book from Oliver's point of view because that would be too long for a letter, but writing about the events in a natural way, picking out the elements that are most interesting.

- Ask: *How will we finish our letter?* (For example: 'See you soon. Love Oliver.')

- Assess the children's ability to use a full sentence, to capture the main points of the story, to write some of the days of the week and to write in the first person.

Differentiation

Support: Instead of writing a full letter, give children postcard-sized pieces of paper with sentences to complete. Tell them to draw Grandpa's garden on the reverse side.
Extension: Expect these children to write a well composed and spelled letter.